# the
# *Beautiful*
## wife  Mentor's Guide

## Sandy Ralya

Kregel
Publications

# Contents

# What It Means to Be a Mentor

Mentoring is a God-idea that works! Satan knows this, and for this reason you may be experiencing some of his lies that cause you to doubt your capability to mentor others. Even now, he may be trying to wreak havoc in your own marriage in an attempt to prevent you from fulfilling the important, God-ordained role of mentor described in Titus 2:3–5. Take heart, dear mentor. Perfection is *not* a requirement! In fact, the struggles you've faced, and continue to face, are the very things God will use to encourage and teach the women you'll mentor.

I should know! Even though I am the founder and director of a mentoring ministry, I continue to experience seasons of difficulty in my marriage that cause me to seek God's face and godly mentoring. As I share my stories of struggles with others, they're heartened with the knowledge that they're not alone in the challenges they face. When we share with each other the details of our journey with God, it's a beautiful thing indeed.

Perfection is not required, but it's important you're trained since as a mentor of wives you play such an important role. The purpose of this mentor's guide is to train and support you as you mentor wives. In this book, you'll discover:

- a short introduction to mentoring that includes what it means to be a mentor as well as practical tips on mentoring a small group;

+ instructions on how to get a Beautiful Womanhood group started;
+ a hostess guide; and
+ a week-by-week leader's guide that coordinates with the content of *The Beautiful Wife*.

But this mentor's guide is just the beginning. As a Beautiful Womanhood mentor you have access to our ministry staff who are here to support your mentoring efforts. If you need any advice, encouragement, or support, please email us at info@beautifulwomanhood.com or call us toll-free at 888.384.5955 and someone will contact you. Because we believe in the power of prayer, our ministry staff also offers to pray for you and the women in your small group by name if you desire.

There are also several online resources that will aid you in living out your commitment to mentor wives:

+ The Beautiful Womanhood blog (www.beautifulwomanhood.com/blog) offers practical, encouraging, biblical reflections written specifically for wives.
+ Bite-size tweets of encouragement for wives are available on Twitter @MentoringWives.
+ Beautiful Womanhood on Facebook (www.facebook.com/beautifulwomanhood) allows you to connect with Sandy and others passionate about becoming beautiful wives.
+ The Beautiful Womanhood Mentors page on Facebook (www.facebook.com/beautifulwomanhoodmentors) offers mentor devotionals and allows you to connect with Sandy and others passionate about mentoring marriage.
+ Beautiful Womanhood seminars provide on-site mentor training with Sandy. Learn more about these seminars on the Church/Ministries page at www.beautifulwomanhood.com.
+ Register your Beautiful Womanhood small group on the Mentor's page of the Beautiful Womanhood website, and gain access to an updated collection of articles, videos, and books

that will enhance your ability to lead discussion on each chapter of *The Beautiful Wife.*

Dear Mentor, you are important to us and vital to the ministry of Beautiful Womanhood, so let us know what you need. God bless you as you embark on this God-ordained journey.

# How to Use This Mentor's Guide

*B*egin by reading "How to Start a Beautiful Womanhood Program" as well as "Mentor Instructions." In these two sections, you'll find everything you need to know before beginning a Beautiful Womanhood small group. If you'll be hosting a group in your home and are interested in learning more about the art of hospitality, you will find the "Hostess Guide" very helpful.

After you establish a small group, you will begin preparing to lead the small group discussion for week 1. If time permits, it would be helpful to establish an introductory meeting where you can get to know each other, share the dates and time you will meet, explain what will happen during a meeting, hand out books if the church has provided them, and assign the reading of chapter 1. Women should be encouraged to consider the Reflection questions at the end of the chapter, though First Steps will not be "assigned" until after the group meets to discuss chapter 1. If time doesn't permit an introductory meeting, communicate by mailing an invitation and following up with a phone call (specific instructions are included in the Hostess Guide). Start out by reading chapter 1 in *The Beautiful Wife*, completing Reflection and First Steps if you haven't done them previously, and then work through the "Week-by-Week Leader's Guide" here in *The Beautiful Wife Mentor's Guide* that corresponds to chapter 1.

Each chapter of the leader's guide is organized into the following sections:

## Before You Meet
### Prayer
The prayers recorded in this guide are written especially for mentors. As you prepare for your group meeting, pray them aloud, and remember each of your mentees by name.

### Introduction
Within each introduction, you'll find information about what you can expect to learn from the week's lesson.

### Discussion Preparation
In this section, you'll be given fresh ideas to jump-start your thoughts as you prepare to lead discussion pertinent to each chapter's topic. Journal your responses in a notebook so you can refer to them during the small group discussion.

## When You Meet
### First Steps Accountability
This is the reminder to share an example of a First Step you've taken since the last meeting, and to ask the women to share any First Steps they've taken.

### Recap
In the recap you'll find a brief summary of each chapter. It is often helpful to read this summary aloud to spark your group's memory and stimulate discussion.

### Points to Emphasize
Most of the group discussion each week will involve talking through the Reflection questions from the end of each chapter. However, particularly significant points that need to be emphasized are mentioned in this section.

### Loving God's Word
Loving, understanding, and implementing God's Word in our daily lives is integral to our success as wives. This section of the leader's

guide focuses on specific Scripture passages that are relevant to each chapter in *The Beautiful Wife*.

### First Steps for Next Time

It's important to take new steps when desiring better results in your life and marriage. At the conclusion of each lesson, direct the women's attention to the First Steps at the end of the *Beautiful Wife* chapter you discussed and tell them you'll follow up at the next meeting to see which steps they've taken and how it's going.

### Creative Touch (Optional)

Though optional, the creative touches listed in this book can meaningfully reinforce the heart of each lesson. If you're feeling creative, you are welcome to come up with your own ideas. Have fun!

# How to Start a Beautiful Womanhood Program

*Your job is to speak out on the things that make for solid doctrine.
. . . Guide older women into lives of reverence so they end up as
neither gossips nor drunks, but models of goodness. By looking at
them, the younger women will know how to love their husbands and
children, be virtuous and pure, keep a good house, be good wives.*
—TITUS 2:1–5 MSG

*One generation will commend your works to another;
they will tell of your mighty acts.*
—PSALM 145:4 NIV

Marriage is hard work! Women around the world have contacted Beautiful Womanhood asking about Beautiful Womanhood small groups in their area. These wives long for encouragement and support on their journey, and they want to develop deep relationships with real women who don't gloss over the dirty realities of life. I'm passionate that their desires be fulfilled, because I was once in their place.

When my marriage was in trouble, I walked into church each Sunday morning desperate for help, but not daring to ask for it because everyone else's marriage seemed so perfect. My life appeared beautiful on the outside, but on the inside it was a mess.

Over time, I turned to God by reading the Bible and praying, and sought guidance from trusted friends, godly mentors, and wise Christian counselors. What I learned transformed my life, and then God did an amazing work in my marriage. The loving support that I received from other women on my own journey inspired me to become the founder and director of Beautiful Womanhood, a Christian mentoring ministry for wives. In 2003, I began holding Beautiful Womanhood seminars where I share my personal testimony of how mentoring strengthened me—and eventually strengthened my marriage—and led me to train other women to be Beautiful Womanhood mentors.

## The Small Group Program

Beautiful Womanhood is a marriage mentoring small group program covering twelve topics relevant to every marriage. Starting Beautiful Womanhood small groups is an exciting and effective way to bring wives together to improve their lives and marriages. If your church already offers small groups, Beautiful Womanhood can be presented as an additional small group option or implemented within an existing small group.

To effectively utilize this program in a church setting, a Beautiful Womanhood coordinator should be assigned to help implement the program, encourage mentors, and be the point-person for any questions. The Beautiful Womanhood coordinator can be the women's ministry leader of the church, a mentor, or a woman who has volunteered specifically for this role. Read more about the role of a Beautiful Womanhood coordinator in the church resources section of www.beautifulwomanhood.com.

Beautiful Womanhood small groups should be limited to no more than six women for every mentor or co-mentoring team. We advise this because of the importance of intimacy in creating effective Beautiful Womanhood small groups. This smaller size allows time for everyone to participate in the discussion. The women get to know each other and often develop friendships.

Once a group is formed, mentors should avoid adding members to the group after the second lesson, even if one member drops out. Adding new members after that will disrupt the intimacy of the group.

The mentor should advise the Beautiful Womanhood coordinator of any changes in the group.

Groups can meet any time, day or night, but mentors should choose a consistent day and time to meet, keeping in mind the schedules of the women who may have children in school. For example, the third Friday of each month at 9:00 a.m. or every Tuesday at 7:00 p.m. You should plan two hours for each lesson, whether or not you choose to provide a snack or meal.

The coordinator can design the Beautiful Womanhood program around whatever schedule and format works best for your church and the women who are participating. The small groups can meet:

+ Once a week for twelve weeks
+ Twice monthly for six months
+ Once a month for a year
+ On a custom schedule that fits within your church calendar year or semester

Churches can implement Beautiful Womanhood in three different formats: home groups, church-hosted meetings, and one-on-one mentoring.

### Home Groups

A home setting is the ideal format for the Beautiful Womanhood program, because it most easily fosters intimacy and trust. Many groups surveyed have chosen to meet in homes and share a meal. The lesson's discussion occurs while eating.

Serving a meal is not mandatory. We encourage doing so because women enjoy sharing a meal together. However, some mentors may choose to serve dessert, or simply provide lemonade and cookies. While food is always a nice touch, it is not the emphasis of Beautiful Womanhood.

The Hostess Guide supplied here provides tips for how to foster a welcoming and hospitable environment. If you'd like time-saving ideas for cooking and hosting, you can find additional hostess helps in the mentor resources section of www.beautifulwomanhood.com.

### Church-Hosted Meetings

Beautiful Womanhood small groups can also be held in a church setting rather than at home. For some mentors, the idea of hosting women in their home seems overwhelming. Along with preparing for the discussion in each lesson, they are concerned about their home's presentability. This is enough to dissuade some potential mentors from mentoring at all. Hosting Beautiful Womanhood groups at church is an effective way to ease mentors into their new role.

Another benefit of church-hosted groups is child care. It may be difficult for women with children to find child care while attending a Beautiful Womanhood small group. The church's nursery facilities can be utilized for those with small children, and the cost of hiring care providers can be divided among those needing child care.

### One-on-One Mentoring

Some women prefer one-on-one mentoring relationships. The Beautiful Womanhood program can be used in this format as well. The instructions for curriculum use are the same. Make sure that the mentor and mentee meet on a regular basis (at least once a month).

## The Curriculum

*The Beautiful Wife* is the curriculum for the Beautiful Womanhood small group program. Each woman participating in the program should have her own copy of the book, and each mentor should also have a copy of *The Beautiful Wife Mentor's Guide*. The participants and mentors should read the applicable chapter, respond to the Reflection questions, and take the First Steps prior to meeting for discussion and fellowship.

Mentors should use the curriculum in the following manner:

+ Open the meeting with prayer.
+ Before beginning the new lesson, hold the women accountable for the last chapter's First Steps, and share any steps you took.
+ Read the Recap summary.
+ Share from your own personal experiences related to the chapter's topic.

+ Discuss the Reflection questions listed at the end of the chapter in *The Beautiful Wife.*
+ Talk about the Points to Emphasize.
+ Follow the instructions for Loving God's Word.
+ After the discussion, encourage your group to take the First Steps (listed after the Reflection questions) and remind them you will hold them accountable at the next meeting for taking First Steps.
+ If you wish, do the Creative Touch activity.
+ End with prayer.

## Mentor Qualifications

I'm often asked to define the qualifications of a Beautiful Womanhood mentor but because every woman's situation is unique, I hesitate to state absolute specifics. Unwilling to discourage any woman sensing God's call to mentor others, please consider the following qualifications as *guidelines.* A potential mentor should pray and ask God to confirm His call on her life. Pastors and women's ministry leaders can provide valuable feedback that will help women know if they are ready to mentor, especially if their age or years of marriage don't fit within these guidelines. A mentor who willingly submits herself to church authority shows great maturity. With that said, here are the guidelines to consider for mentors:

+ Actively seeking God in daily devotions
+ Regular church attendee
+ Married at least fifteen years
+ Aged forty-plus

## Additional Resources

The appendix to *The Beautiful Wife* includes a list of suggested reading for each chapter. To further develop your knowledge on a given topic, consider reading one of the recommended resources listed there.

*The Beautiful Wife Prayer Journal* is an optional companion book to *The Beautiful Wife* curriculum. It is not required, but is highly recommended for additional enrichment. It provides a place to give birth to faith, inspiration, and revelation for you, the women in your group, and your marriages. After reading a chapter in *The Beautiful Wife*, you can record your responses, reflections, and requests in the corresponding chapter of *The Beautiful Wife Prayer Journal*. You may choose to provide an opportunity in the small group discussion for anyone to share any thoughts or revelations from their journal. However, the journaling itself should take place before each meeting.

If you've already completed a *Beautiful Wife Prayer Journal* as a mentee, I recommend that you start a new, separate journal each time you work through this study as a mentor. As you re-encounter questions that you answered previously, whether a month or a year or more ago, compare your answers with what you wrote the last time. How does your response today differ from the first time you read *The Beautiful Wife* and considered the question? If you've seen progress in this area of your life, you can provide helpful encouragement to those you are mentoring. If you have not seen progress, prayerfully reflect on why that's the case. You can still be an encouragement to others as you share your ongoing struggles in certain areas and display a desire to keep pursuing growth.

Visit mentor resources at www.beautifulwomanhood.com or www .facebook.com/beautifulwomanhoodmentors for additional resources to help you lead discussion for each chapter in *The Beautiful Wife* and ongoing encouragement from the Beautiful Womanhood ministry staff.

# Mentor Instructions

Today's women are looking for mentors to guide them through the choices that affect their life and marriage. I know because they've contacted me from around the world, inquiring about Beautiful Womanhood small groups in their area.

I'm passionate for their search to be rewarded because I was, am, and always will be a woman desiring mentoring relationships. That's right. I *have* and *will continue* to rely on godly mentoring. Mentoring has helped me navigate all the hills and valleys that my marriage has traveled for more than thirty years—and it will continue to help me.

Gathering with other women in a safe place allows each woman to ask those *But how? What if?* questions, and experience all the benefits community offers. When women take time to teach each other godly principles and share personal struggles and successes, they stand on the frontlines to strengthen marriages and protect families.

The apostle Paul wrote about the need for marriage mentoring: "These older women must train the younger women to love their husbands and their children, to live wisely and be pure, to take care of their homes, to do good, and to be submissive to their husbands. Then they will not bring shame on the word of God" (Titus 2:4–5). Paul knew, under the inspiration of the Holy Spirit, that women need women. When women come together, beautiful things can happen!

I once spoke to a small group of young women on the topic of mystique and afterward answered their questions concerning the Beautiful Womanhood program. At the conclusion a woman came up to me, her eyes shining with tears, and said, "Thank you for not forgetting about us." It was a thrill I won't soon forget. She and many other married women are working to beat the odds and experience fulfillment in marriage, and she was grateful I met her on the front-lines with help. I felt such purpose, and you will too, as you share what your experiences and God's Word have taught you.

It's one thing to develop a healthy marriage; it's another thing to mentor a woman into a healthier marriage. So, I want to give you everything you need to support your God-given call to mentor, because you are the heart and soul of the Beautiful Womanhood ministry. We are all grateful for your obedience to Titus 2:3–5. As you step out in faith, God is pleased and we are cheering for you!

Remember, we invite you to register at the Mentor Page of the Beautiful Womanhood website, where you will find encouragement as well as additional resources (YouTube videos, magazine articles, blog posts, etc.) that will aid your ability to communicate each chapter's message to your small group. Once you register, you will also have access to a Beautiful Womanhood Mentor Consultant who would love to hear from you and pray with you. All questions, concerns, and feedback are welcomed.

You can also connect with and ask questions of Beautiful Woman-hood staff and other mentors by joining the Beautiful Womanhood Mentors page on Facebook.

Please keep in touch and share your mentoring experiences with us. The Beautiful Womanhood ministry and the mentors who follow in your footsteps can learn from your knowledge. God bless you!

## Weapons for the Frontlines

Marriage is under attack and the battle lines have been drawn: God upholds His creation of marriage and desires its health and preservation, while Satan desires to kill, steal, and destroy the unity between husbands and wives. As a mentor, you're entering the battlefield to reclaim marriage for God's glory, so you'll need effective "weapons" to spoil the enemy's plans.

### Honesty

Since part of my ministry is to encourage women into mentoring relationships, you could probably guess I am passionate about women sharing personal experiences. What you might not guess was that, for a long time, I resisted sharing my personal weaknesses. Unfortunately, by placing a glamorous spin on my past, I made it difficult for my audience to connect with me.

When I led one of my first Beautiful Womanhood seminars, I gave an account of my marriage's first eleven difficult years. I shared my journey: how I learned to listen to and obey God's instructions to women in His Word. I shared my revelation: when we do what only we can do, God does what we cannot. I told them how God transformed me over time, how He transformed my husband, and how we recommitted our marriage vows on our twelfth anniversary, praising God for all He had done! I finished with "And now my marriage is in the heights!" I always was one for the dramatic.

But the truth was, my husband Tom and I went through more struggles between the renewal of our vows and the infamous "heights" statement. In fact, we still encounter difficulty from time to time—all marriages do. At the time of that seminar, things were going smoothly, but not long afterward, Tom and I were back in the valley, dreaming of the heights. As the years go on, we're still learning from the valleys and the heights. I'm grateful—albeit reluctantly at times—for the lessons that further conform me to God's image, lessons I can share with others.

Glossing over my marriage's current issues offered little encouragement to those at the seminar who were slogging through the valley. Worse, my dramatic "everything is perfect" statement could have discouraged my listeners; and discouragement often leads to hopelessness. These are sad results for my good intentions.

Perhaps you too have been tempted to control what you reveal about yourself and your marriage in order to portray a more acceptable image. Fear and pride keep many people from being completely truthful. I know from experience. As the leader of a marriage mentoring ministry, I sometimes worry about what people would think if they knew Tom and I still encountered difficulty. Would they reject my teaching? Would I fail in my desire to communicate the necessity and benefits of marriage mentoring? Would they think less of me?

So as you prepare to mentor wives, it's important to remind yourself of two things: one, we all struggle; two, struggles do not disqualify us from helping others. Remember that Christ's strength is made perfect in our weakness. God isn't looking for perfect women, but for those who trust in His Word and are totally dependent on Him. From this dependent position, His power will flow through you to accomplish great things in your life as well as in the lives of those you mentor.

I've seen over and over again that my honesty ignites honesty in others and causes them to look within their own hearts. This is exciting—it's the first step to healing and real change within a woman. I didn't experience this kind of deep connection with my seminar audience when I glossed over the realities of struggle in my life and marriage. It's been a humbling, exhilarating experience to become more honest in my seminars. John 8:32 says, "And you will know the truth, and the truth will set you free."

Stories are the best part of any teaching. As you mentor, share *your* stories—not mine. The women in your group want to hear about *your* experiences. Think back to all the big and little incidents that have occurred throughout the life of your marriage. Have you struggled to show respect for your husband when you disagreed with his behavior? Do you experience frustration with family members when you've overcommitted yourself? Is sex often at the bottom of your priority list? Take time during the week to get in touch with these stories and share them at the group meeting! Tell on yourself. Drag your stories out of the closet, dust them off if you have to, and tell them with the knowledge that others will be glad you did.

Most of the women you mentor will be honest in direct proportion to the level of honesty you portray. As the leader, your honesty sets the level of intimacy your group can experience. Make sure your stories focus on you (not your husband) with an emphasis on what the Holy Spirit taught or is teaching you through struggle or success. In this way, you are setting an example for those you mentor to follow.

### Godliness

Without a personal relationship with Jesus Christ and a knowledge that listening to and obeying His Word has made a profound difference in your life, mentors have nothing to offer those struggling to find their way. The health of your relationship with God will strengthen your ability to mentor.

Be advised! *Health* is not a synonym for *perfection*. A healthy relationship with God is characterized by growth. Grow your relationship with Jesus by reading the Bible, praying, and living out of the knowledge that God loves you unconditionally even though you're not perfect (nor ever will be until heaven).

Remember, whatever you're focused on will grow, and growth in godliness will help you mentor others. What you learn and experience in your relationship with Him will provide the food with which you feed the hungry wives around your table—spiritual food that will satisfy.

Mentors have learned—and are still learning—to walk out godly principles in a practical way. This wisdom and experience has the potential to make a powerful impact on those we mentor.

### Prayer

Because you know Jesus, you have learned the importance of prayer. As a Beautiful Womanhood mentor, it is important to pray for God's guidance and blessing on your group.

One mentor became very nervous before her first group meeting and wondered what she had gotten herself into. Remembering her mentor training, she sat down to pray. She felt somewhat better before the women arrived. Afterward, she was amazed at how well it went and knew God had provided her with what she needed. Other mentors have also testified to the same blessing.

In Matthew 7, Jesus talks about effective prayer. He exhorts us to keep asking, keep knocking, and keep seeking so that we will find and receive the help we need. In Matthew 18:19 Jesus tells us this: "If two of you agree down here on earth concerning anything you ask, my Father in heaven will do it for you." Pray with your husband concerning the women in your group. Together, ask God to bless them and their marriages.

### Love

Knowing Jesus also means looking at those you mentor through the eyes of God. Some women in your group may be difficult to love.

In *A Love Worth Giving*, Max Lucado writes that, in these situations, it is necessary to go to God and fill yourself with His love before you can give out to those difficult to love. When we remind ourselves that God loves us even when we don't deserve it, our ability to love others is enhanced.

You are a vessel through which God can wrap His loving arms around a woman difficult for others to love. The young women you mentor may have never before experienced this unconditional love. This is an amazing opportunity to extend grace to one of God's children. Considering 1 Corinthians 13 as it would apply to you as a mentor, let me offer this encouragement: Let love be your highest goal and the motive behind your every word and action. Without it, all the knowledge you share—meaningless noise; the gifts you bring to the mentoring table—no good to anyone; and any sacrifices you make—no value whatsoever. There are three things that will endure—faith, hope, and love—and the greatest of these is love.

### The Holy Spirit

Before the women come and also throughout the time you spend together, be sensitive to the Spirit. Listen for His promptings.

One mentor shared that as she was busily preparing for the women in her group to come, the Spirit spoke to her heart saying, "I want you to be Mary, not Martha." With dishes still in the sink, and laundry in full view stacked on the dryer, she stopped all physical preparations and began preparing her own heart by spending time with God. After the group left, she recognized the breakthrough moments that had happened in the women's hearts. A coincidence? I think not. Having first submitted herself to the Holy Spirit, the women in her group followed suit. Full of the Spirit, you will be a vessel through which the Spirit will spill over onto the lives of the women you mentor.

The Spirit will also guide you to highlight certain points during group discussion. Just because you are familiar with a concept related to marriage doesn't mean those you mentor are. They might not know anything about something that you take for granted. Share things you sense the Spirit placing on your heart.

When the Holy Spirit controls our lives, He will produce His kind of fruit in us: love, joy, peace, patience, kindness, goodness, faithfulness, gentleness, and self-control (Galatians 5:22–23). These gifts will prove useful as you mentor on the frontlines.

## Effective Co-Mentoring

You may decide to partner with another woman and co-mentor your Beautiful Womanhood small group. The vast majority of women who co-mentor find it a blessing. Two women bring different strengths to the group—one may be blessed with the gift of hospitality, while another may have the gift of teaching. You may even choose to alternate responsibilities and homes.

Co-mentors also bring two God-given personalities and perspectives to the women they mentor. You each have different life experiences to draw from which will connect with different women in your group. If questions come up within your group that one of you can't relate to, your co-mentor may have the experience needed to make a connection. However, even in co-mentoring situations there will be times when neither of you will know what to say. Don't be ashamed to admit you don't have an answer. Only God knows the answers to all things.

## Time Management Tips

Your time—and the time of women you are mentoring—is valuable, so you'll want to make your mentoring time as productive as possible. When you mentor, turn off your cell phone and answer phone calls later. Ask the women to turn off or silence their phones as well. If you are serving a meal as part of the small group, eat soon after the women arrive and try to start the discussion portion promptly at a designated time. If one woman is habitually late, start without her. You will actually be helping her by training her to be more responsible. End with prayer on time. It is better that the women in your group wish they could have stayed longer than for them to wonder when it will end.

## Respecting Family Members

It is important to keep the tone of the discussion positive. No water-cooler-husband-bashing allowed! Beautiful Womanhood groups are a time to honestly discuss problems and issues, but you must help your group maintain a balance of communicating honestly without belittling their husbands. Always remain loyal to the family members represented by the group.

Address the subject of gossip when the group first meets, and do so again if gossip surfaces at a later time. One mentor shared these words at her first meeting:

> This group is designed to help women grow spiritually, relationally, emotionally, and physically. The comments and questions that are discussed in the group should pertain to how the book's message is affecting you and how you can grow through what you are learning. It's not about your neighbor, sister, friend, parents, cousin, etc. This is about YOU and God. Furthermore, it is important that you honor your husband by what you say in the group. There should be no criticisms made about your spouse in the group. Instead, consider your godly response to those things that pertain to your relationship with your spouse.

## Confidentiality

Confidentiality within the group is important. What is said in the group stays in the group. You may have to remind group members of this from time to time.

However, if someone in your group discloses information concerning illegalities or suggests that someone is causing real harm to themselves or others, keeping this information to yourself isn't helpful. Privately and lovingly confront the woman, letting her know that by remaining silent, she is enabling sin to continue unchecked. Encourage her to go to the proper authorities for help. If she refuses, contact your pastor, a licensed psychologist, or law enforcement official for help in processing the information you've been privy to.

## Potential Problems
### No-Shows

When members of my group missed a meeting for one reason or another, I began to wonder if they weren't enjoying or benefiting from

24

our time together. I was very discouraged at times. I pushed past this discouragement by reminding myself that mentoring is about obeying God—it's not about me! This knowledge freed me to focus on each woman who came, not on the ones who didn't.

A woman I know felt the Spirit's prompting to mentor wives and wanted to offer a Beautiful Womanhood group to the women in her neighborhood. They were all excited to begin, but when the time came to start, everyone had excuses as to why they couldn't come. Discouraged, she wondered if she had heard God at all.

Soon after, while participating in a prayer meeting at her children's school, some of the mothers began talking about the struggles they were experiencing in their marriages. Again, she felt the prompting of the Spirit and so she invited them to a Beautiful Womanhood group. They all came, and their lives and marriages are being changed! Though things didn't turn out as she'd initially anticipated, God is moving through her obedience.

### Adding Members

Once your group is set and you start meeting, do not add members after the second lesson, even if one member drops out. Adding new members will disrupt the intimacy of the group.

If anyone drops out of your group early on, you should call your church coordinator. There may be a waiting list of young women wanting to join a Beautiful Womanhood group.

### A Dominating Talker

When you mentor a group, there is usually one talkative woman who will tend to dominate the conversation. When this happens, turn away from the woman and ask someone else, "What has been your experience?" or "What do you think?" If necessary, you may have to speak with "the talker" after the group meeting. Make sure your correction is positive. For example: "I appreciate your willing participation, but I'm concerned that other women who are more timid are not speaking up. I'd like to be sure that every woman has equal voice in our meetings. If you could make a point of holding back, that'd prompt other women to speak up."

It can be difficult to confront her, but the success of the group is at stake. Do it for the sake of the others. If you don't lead, someone else will. God has chosen you for this position—ask Him for strength to grow in leadership skills.

### Child Care

If you have young children at home, arrange for someone to care for them during the group meeting. It is not your job to provide child care for the women in your group. We recommend you convey to your group that they are responsible for finding someone to care for their children. We have found that women are more than happy to get a sitter in order to spend time with a mentor.

### Politics, Books, and Church Theology

The second time my Beautiful Womanhood small group met just happened to be the day before a national election. My enthusiasm for my candidate spilled over after the group discussion and I made it clear who I was voting for and why. I knew I shouldn't do it, but I did anyway. It slipped out! I realized I needed to set things right and did so by apologizing at the next meeting. The women were gracious and I learned a valuable lesson: Keep your mouth closed when it comes to politics, you never know who you might offend and why.

This same rule applies to books and theology. Everyone has a different opinion about these things. Beautiful Womanhood mentors are focused on helping wives grow and strengthen their marriage, and that's a big enough focus to keep you occupied without bringing up controversial issues.

If you make a slip like I did, apologize as soon as possible. You'll be setting a good example for those you mentor.

### Pets

If you are hosting the group at your house and you have pets, plan to have your pets out of the way—either in a closed room or outside—when women start arriving. It never fails; the one person who does not care for animals will be the one person your dog will gravitate toward. Many women also have allergies to pets, so it is courteous and hospitable to keep them away from the group while it is meeting. Warn women in advance, so they can take allergy medication if they need to do so.

### Smoking and Alcohol

There should be no smoking during the group meetings. Please do not serve alcoholic beverages.

### Sensitive Information

When women come together and share, difficult issues may arise in your discussion. As the group becomes more intimate, this possibility increases. Many women have not experienced intimacy with other women, and when they find themselves in a loving, warm environment, they are apt to disclose hurts.

One mentor shared that a woman in her group revealed she had been sexually molested as a child. The mentor placed her hand on the woman's arm and said how sorry she was and that she understood that experience would make trusting her husband more difficult. After the meeting, the mentor called her Beautiful Womanhood coordinator who instructed her to call the woman, ask how she felt having shared this personal information within the group, and affirm her decision to do so.

It's important you're aware that in an intimate setting, sensitive information will come out. And that's a good thing. Once disclosed, healing is possible. If the situation is extremely personal and something the group is not equipped to handle, ask the woman if you can speak to her after the meeting. Tell her you are glad she shared her situation, and pray with her, asking the Holy Spirit to guide you to the next step. Your role as a Beautiful Womanhood mentor is to lovingly lead this woman to help and safety.

### Referring for Professional Help

If you encounter a situation you are not equipped to handle, suggest to the woman that she seek additional help from a pastor or professional counselor. If she is in great need, be prepared to refer her immediately. The names and numbers of a few pastors and counselors is important information to have on hand before your mentoring group begins. Contact your Beautiful Womanhood coordinator for this information (if you are mentoring within a church), or check out reputable Christian counseling services in your community.

Are you wondering what you've gotten yourself into? Don't worry. Mentoring is a God-idea. Your job is to obey God's call to mentor. He promises to stay with you, work through you, and make all things turn out for the good of those who love Him. The women you mentor will be blessed by you, and you will be blessed by them—but you don't have to take my word for it. As you read the stories below from four women who have been mentored or were mentors, ask God to speak to your heart regarding how He'll use you to bless other women, and how you'll be blessed in the process.

### A MENTOR'S STORY OF LOVE

A few months ago, I was getting a pedicure when an older woman walked in. She had a lovely, sensitive face. I wondered, *Is she a Christian?* As she sat down, her friend said, "I'll pick you up in an hour, Twila."

The name rang a bell. I mentioned to her that the only Twila I'd known had had a great influence on me. She said she'd love to hear about her, so I told her about my first grade teacher.

In first grade, I was an unhappy, introverted little girl. Adopted a year and a half earlier, I rarely smiled. Malnutrition and abuse had scarred my past and built invisible walls around my heart. My teacher helped tear down those walls with simple, loving acts. She brushed my hair during recess. She hugged me. She held my hand. She even took me out for supper with her husband. I experienced love in her presence. She told me that Jesus loved me, too. Because of her love, I'd never forgotten her.

I told the woman beside me that I had come to realize what it was that had impacted me so greatly: it was the love, purpose, and hope my teacher had offered me. I longed to meet my teacher again and tell her what she meant to me.

Twila asked, "Is your name Debbie Boersma?"

I was astonished. "Yes."

Tears were in her eyes. "I was your first grade teacher."

Words cannot express what transpired in the moments following our discovery, but needless to say it was quite a reunion!

When I think about Twila, and how she influenced me, I think of those I have an opportunity to influence. The women I mentor today need the same things I did in first grade. They need to know that they are loved, they have purpose in their roles as women, and there is hope for their future. As Beautiful Womanhood mentors, we have an opportunity to give these gifts every time we meet with them. We can love them right where they are and let them know of their significance to God, in the world, in their family, and within the group. We can let them know they have purpose. We can speak of hope in Jesus. What a difference we can make in their lives. Maybe we will never know how much a difference.

Because of Twila, I approached the next years in my life with renewed hope! We as Christians have the best to offer others through Jesus Christ. I'm grateful to be a mentor and be able to pass on what I have been given.

—*Deborah H.*, MENTOR


## A MENTOR'S STORY OF PURPOSE

I had been praying for a way to connect with the younger generation in my church. Many marriages were struggling, and I wanted to help in a practical way. When I heard about the Beautiful Womanhood program, I knew God wanted to establish this marriage mentoring program in my church. As the Women's Ministry leader, I knew it would be an effective tool in the lives of women. I've enjoyed teaching the women the godly principles found in each lesson and watching the growth in their lives. We enjoy our time together so much! This is the third year I've participated in the program, hosting Beautiful Womanhood luncheons in my home. My favorite part? The thrill of having younger women come up to me at church and thank me for the investment I've made in their lives.

—*Donna T., mentor*

### A Mentored Woman's Story of Hope

My name is Dorie Barron, and I am a beautiful woman! I couldn't make this statement without stumbling over it three years ago. After one year in the Beautiful Womanhood program, *I can!* God used Beautiful Womanhood to do a tremendous work in my marriage and my life, and it continues to this day.

In the Beautiful Womanhood group, I learned how to show respect for my husband in practical ways, how not to be his mother, how to have God's best for our marriage. I learned how to invite romance, how to open the lines of communication, and how to develop my mystique. If you are thinking, "What's mystique? Do I have any of that?" then you need to join a Beautiful Womanhood group!

My husband loves Beautiful Womanhood just as much as I do. He did all he could to make sure that I attended every luncheon because he knew what a difference it was making in our lives. I was encouraged personally as well.

My fellow mentees are my closest friends and prayer partners. We share each other's burdens, love each other's kids, and pray for each other's husbands. I know that I would not be where I am today if it wasn't for their friendship. Our mentor was awesome for opening up her home and heart to a group of strangers who were the most chatty group ever, I do believe! She poured godly wisdom and love into us each month. Going to our luncheon was like going on a vacation—relaxing atmosphere, beautifully set table, no kids, no peanut butter and jelly or mac and cheese. Sometimes we even had two forks! I could talk for hours about how awesome it was.

I am beautiful because I have allowed myself to be teachable. I learned from *The Beautiful Wife*, my mentor, and my friends in the group. I am beautiful because I am connected to other beautiful women. I am beautiful because each day I come closer to God and to being the woman He has called me to be.

—DORIE B., MENTEE

## A MENTORED WOMAN'S STORY OF HEALING

As a young married woman, I heard good teaching about marriage in church but didn't dare ask questions or share my marriage struggles with others because I thought everyone else's marriage seemed so good. Consequently, I suffered in silence because it was difficult for me to trust others with the messy reality of my marriage.

Fortunately, God placed many godly women in my life who spent time with me, cared about me, and showed me unconditional love. Their love was the chisel God used to break my silence. Once I started talking, a flood of emotional pain began to overflow. Their feedback to the ugly events I'd suffered helped me see that my marriage was full of emotional abuse—something I hadn't seen on my own. My blindness to this fact was the equivalent of "not seeing the forest for the trees." Because abuse was an issue in my marriage, I was advised to seek professional help—which I did.

Godly mentoring and Christian counseling created a hunger in me to know God's truth concerning my marriage. I began to dig into the Word and learned that Tom wasn't the only one sinning in our relationship. My response to his sin was equally displeasing to God and something I alone was responsible for. In fact, it was the only part of my marriage that was actually within my control. This fact empowered me to make personal changes that restored my dignity and served as one of the tools God used to break up the hard places of Tom's heart.

I credit mentoring with illuminating the fact of my need for professional help. Mentoring also helped me fit the puzzle pieces of God's Word and counseling together to create a beautiful picture of His redemption in my life and eventually in my marriage.

—SANDY RALYA, MENTEE AND MENTOR

*Dear Lord, bless this mentor with the special favor You give in Christ Jesus as she teaches and shares the things You've revealed to her throughout the years of her marriage. Give her ears to hear what Your Spirit is saying. Place in her mouth the words You want her to speak. Ignite her heart with the power to comprehend Your great love for her so she can give out of the overflow. Protect her and her marriage as she fights in the battle to strengthen marriages, loving each woman You bring to her group for Your glory. Amen!*

# Hostess Guide

## by Angela Pleune

*Do not forget or neglect or refuse to extend hospitality to strangers [in the brotherhood—being friendly, cordial, and gracious, sharing the comforts of your home and doing your part generously], for through it some have entertained angels without knowing it.*
—HEBREWS 13:2 (AMP)

*As a general rule, a home should not have to be rearranged, redecorated, or refurbished for entertaining, because it is already expressive and interesting, simply by force of the people who live there.*
—MARTHA STEWART

This hostess guide is meant to help you focus on creating a warm atmosphere for the women in your small group. The most important thing to remember is that the women you mentor will be blessed by the investment you make in their lives. Whether you serve coffee and cookies, lemonade, or a light meal, it can be nurturing if offered in love.

Fostering the right atmosphere for your Beautiful Womanhood small group is an important aspect of preparing your lesson. A woman who does not feel welcome or comfortable will not be able to listen and learn, much less open up or ask questions. As the hostess, you are in control of making your guests feel relaxed and, ultimately, in control of the success of the meeting. You'll want to create an atmosphere which is welcoming, comfortable, and beautiful.

## Create a Welcoming Atmosphere

I recommend sending personal invitations to the women in your group a couple of weeks before your group's first meeting. The invitations can be handmade, store bought, or printed out. Make sure to include your address, phone number, date, and time on the invitation. If you are planning to serve a meal or light refreshments, include mention of that in the invitation as well. Include a reminder to read the first chapter in *The Beautiful Wife* before the meeting and to consider the Reflection questions. (First Steps won't be "assigned" until the group meets to discuss chapter 1.) If your church isn't providing each woman's book, let her know where books can be purchased. Everyone loves to receive fun mail. This will stir excitement about your first meeting.

Call the women in your group two days before your first meeting. Tell them you are excited about them coming. Inquire about allergies—food (to aid you in food preparation), pet (to forewarn them if necessary), seasonal (so you know if fresh-cut lilacs are a bad idea, for instance), or others (such as scented candles). There's nothing less welcoming than a home that causes a guest to have an allergic reaction! Then, ask if they need directions to your home, and tell them where to park. Ask if they have any other questions.

There are several benefits to this phone contact. You will have a final head-count for preparation, and if someone is no longer planning on attending, you can let your church coordinator know. You will stir their excitement and let them know you are looking forward to spending time with them. I guarantee they will be counting down the days to come and spend time with you because you have made them feel welcome.

## Create a Comfortable Atmosphere

Comfort begins at the door. Greet each guest at the door when she arrives. Take her coat. To help set the mood, have soft music playing. Being the first to arrive can be daunting, especially if women do not know each other well, and the music can help fill awkward silence. You can leave the music playing softly during your meeting or turn it off when everyone arrives.

Since some women are early, some are on time, and some are behind schedule, the early guests will be waiting. Make them comfortable by inviting them into the kitchen and offering them warm cider, sparkling water, lemonade, or coffee. Your hospitality will help them feel more relaxed and comfortable.

Do not make apologies for your home. Apologizing tells others that you are uncomfortable with the setting, so they should be uncomfortable too. Before the women arrive, prepare your attitude by thanking God for your home, including the stained carpet and unfinished paint job. Opening your home when it is not at its best makes you faithful in small things and shows God you are content with what you have. It also speaks volumes to the young women who may not have large or finished homes and encourages them to entertain at home also.

Comfortable entertaining centers around organization and a relaxed hostess. The more organized and relaxed you are, the more at-ease your guests will be. When everything is ready on time, you have created an atmosphere prepared for ministry.

## Create a Beautiful Atmosphere

The purpose of Beautiful Womanhood groups is to convince women to appreciate and exercise their God-given beauty as imitators of Christ. The beauty women find in your home should support that purpose. As you welcome women into your home, and invite them to know you on a deeper level, your home will reveal something of yourself and your values. Creating beauty for your guests should focus on three areas: personal style, seasonal inspiration, and special touches.

Your personal style is an expression of your uniqueness. For tips on determining and expressing your personal style at home, refer to chapter 10 in *The Beautiful Wife*, "Creating a Culture of Beauty."

Seasonal inspiration is one of the best ways to create beauty in your home, as it highlights God's beautiful creation. The seasons inspire my decorating: colors, a centerpiece, and sometimes candles.

Just one look at the flowers blooming in the yard, or a visit to the local flower shop will stir your appreciation of God's creativity. A simple, seasonal centerpiece can be a bowl of clementines at the holidays, fresh tulips in the spring, small potted herbs in summer, or pumpkins and leaves in autumn. It should not be expensive or elaborate. It should be something you love.

Special touches are little extras that let your guests know that they are special to you, but these extras do not have to appear every time your group meets. A special touch could be a small gift or special food. My Beautiful Womanhood mentor once added a chocolate bar to each place setting, wrapped in valentine paper, for us to take home as a gift. Other favors include little ornaments, small bags of candy, a single flower, or a wrapped candle. If you notice a woman does not have *The Beautiful Wife Prayer Journal*, you could consider giving a copy to her as a gift to help enrich her study.

Opening your home for your Beautiful Womanhood small group is a wonderful way to nurture women and build close relationships.

Please refer to the Mentors page of our website if you would like to provide a meal during your Beautiful Womanhood small group. Helpful and detailed instructions for doing so are included.

# Week-by-Week Leader's Guide

This week-by-week guide will walk you through the extra preparation you need to be ready to lead discussion for each chapter of *The Beautiful Wife*. Complete the "Before You Meet" section prayerfully and reflectively so you are well prepared. Get acquainted with the "When You Meet" section and refer back to it during the group discussion. The appendix of *The Beautiful Wife* includes a suggested reading list to further develop your knowledge on a given topic.

Each Beautiful Womanhood small group meeting should follow this simple format:

- Open the meeting with prayer. *less than 5 minutes*
- Before beginning a discussion of the current lesson, hold the women accountable for the First Steps of the previous lesson. Share about any steps you took and how it turned out, then ask them to share their experiences. *about 10 minutes*
- Recap the current chapter. *less than 5 minutes*
- Share from your personal experiences related to the current chapter's topic. (The notes you journal during the Discussion Preparation section of the guide will prepare you for this sharing time.) *less than 5 minutes*
- Discuss the Reflection questions listed at the end of the week's current chapter. (If you don't have time for every question, be especially sure to cover everything in the Points to Emphasize section of the guide.) *45–60 minutes*

+ Follow the instructions in the Loving God's Word section of the guide. *about 10 minutes*
+ After the discussion, encourage your group to take the First Steps (listed after the Reflection questions) in the current chapter, and remind them you will hold them accountable for doing so at the next meeting. Mention the importance of taking new steps in order to experience better results in marriage. After all, isn't that why they have made time to study *The Beautiful Wife*? *less than 5 minutes*
+ If you wish, you can do the Creative Touch activity. *varies*
+ End with prayer. *about 10 minutes*

─────────────── CHAPTER ONE ───────────────

## Equipping for the Journey

### Before You Meet
#### Prayer

*Dear Lord, thank You for the opportunity to share my journey as a wife with the women in my Beautiful Womanhood group. Give me the courage to be honest about my own faults and failures for the benefit of others. In Jesus' name, I renounce a spirit of fear that would cause me to self-protect. Fill my mouth with Holy Spirit–inspired words to bless and support these women. Remind me of stories I can share that will encourage the women that they're not alone in what they face. Plant this foundational message of turning to God, understanding our role, and sharing in a community of women deep within our hearts so it will bear fruit in all our marriages—even a hundred-fold! For the praise of Your glorious grace, amen.*

### Introduction

You embarked on a crucial role when you made the decision to mentor wives. I'm grateful for your passion for others that has responded to the Holy Spirit's prompting. God loves you and desires to work through you so other women can experience longevity and fulfillment in marriage, which gives great testimony to God's love and faithfulness.

We all know that without a strong foundation, the structure built upon it won't last. The same is true of marriage. Unless the foundation is solid, the promise of longevity is improbable and brokenness is inevitable. The first chapter of *The Beautiful Wife* is foundational and therefore key to understanding the approach to be taken in each successive chapter. "Equipping for the Journey" discusses the tools needed for becoming a beautiful wife—turning to God, understanding your role, and sharing within a community of women. These tools will help you and the women in your group navigate well through the next eleven lessons, as well as through all the marital hills and valleys you and those you mentor will encounter throughout married life.

I've been married since 1980 and I still rely on these principles. While on vacation in 2011, I was struggling with a recurring issue that had plagued my marriage for five years. Addicted to thinking through my problem, my thoughts were in turmoil and our unity was deteriorating. One day I felt prompted to take an early morning walk, and while I was out, the Holy Spirit arrested my tumultuous thoughts. His words? "Sandy, be still and worship Me." In other words, turn to God. Once I was still, He spoke again. "What would you say to another woman in this position?" I knew the answer immediately—I would tell her, "Go get help!" In other words, share within community. When I returned home, I shared my struggle with mentors and a Christian counselor. While in community, my role in the problem was revealed and I was able to make much-needed adjustments in my thoughts and actions, which ultimately increased unity between Tom and me. Turning to God, understanding your role, and sharing within community are effective marriage-building tools.

### Discussion Preparation

During the first meeting, it's vital that you discard a glittering image you may be tempted to project in order to protect your self-image. If you succumb to this fleshly tendency of protecting your image, the women in your group won't be able to relate to your apparent perfection, and worse, they will become discouraged when comparing their marriage to yours. The level of transparency you exhibit at this first meeting will set the tone for the rest of your time together.

To prepare for the discussion, respond to the Reflection questions at the end of chapter 1, "Equipping for the Journey." Record your response in a journal or note book, so you can refer to your notes during the discussion. In addition to the Reflection questions, journal a response to the following prompts:

+ Describe any "aha" moments that have come through the reading of Scripture, giving you the very direction you needed. Share the passage(s) that inspired you. Emphasize the importance of recording these verses in a prayer journal where they can be read or prayed when needed.
+ Share about a particular incident when being vulnerable within a godly community of women encouraged you to make changes that impacted your marriage. (Flip ahead and read chapter 3 "Living as the Genuine Article" in *The Beautiful Wife* if you need further encouragement in this area of vulnerability.)

## When You Meet
### Recap
Marriage is all about becoming one, but making that happen is difficult when your husband's rough edges are grating on your own. With so many marriages failing, one wonders whether it's even possible to grow and sustain a healthy marriage. Where can a woman turn for help? In the book of Titus we find God-inspired, success-driven tools for helping wives adapt to this challenging role: Turn to God, understand your role, and share within a community of women.

### Points to Emphasize
During the first lesson, communicate to the women in your group that you will discuss each chapter's message using the foundation-laying principles found in "Equipping for the Journey." Turning to

God, understanding your role, and sharing within a community of women aren't just beautiful ideals but are powerful tools that enable you to lay a strong foundation for marriage. Disregarding these principles will cause you sorrow, disillusionment, and a lack of fulfillment in your marriage.

### Loving God's Word

Share any Scriptures you have found during your daily reading of the Bible that pertain to you, your husband, and your marriage. Encourage group members to do the same by sharing answers to your Scripture-inspired prayers.

### First Steps for Next Time

Remind the women to take the First Steps on page 38 and let them know you'll be asking them which steps they've taken at your next meeting. Each week, mention the importance of taking new steps in order to experience better results in marriage. After all, isn't that why you've made time to study *The Beautiful Wife*?

### Creative Touch (Optional)

Prepare this bookmark (you can either photocopy or re-create it), laminate it, punch a hole in the top and add a decorative ribbon if you'd like, and give one to each woman. This visually reminds women how to approach every problem or concern in their marriage.

## FIRST STEPS

Read the Bible every day —even if only one verse. Pray for your husband every day! Thank God for your marriage.

*Dear God, thank you for my husband. Help me to see him the way You do. Encourage my husband to love You with all his heart, soul, mind, and strength. Remind me to turn to You first when I don't know what to do. As I read the Bible and pray, help me to understand my role as a wife. Fill me with patience as I wait for YOUR guidance and answers to my prayers. Please give me the courage to share openly and honestly with the women who surround me so I can be strengthened with love, purpose, and hope. In Jesus' name, amen.*

### Leading Someone to Christ

Before concluding this lesson, share the basic points of the gospel with your group:

1. God wants you to experience abundant peace and eternal life because He loves you. (Romans 5:1; John 3:16; 10:10)
2. But we've got a problem. God has given us free will and doesn't make us choose Him and His ways. But we've all chosen sin and this has caused a separation between us and God. All our attempts to bridge this gap have failed miserably. (Romans 3:23; 6:23; Isaiah 59:2; Proverbs 14:12)
3. God has a plan that spans the gap. The cross of Jesus Christ is the only answer to this problem—the bridge that connects us. He died on the cross, which paid the penalty for our sins, and then rose from the grave. (1 Timothy 2:5; 1 Peter 3:18; Romans 5:8)
4. To receive Christ, we must trust in Him by expressing personal acceptance of His payment for our sins. (Revelation 3:20; John 1:12; Romans 10:9)

Ask if anyone would like to accept Jesus Christ as their personal Lord and Savior. Don't assume everyone in your group has. If someone responds to your question, be prepared to lead them in a prayer by saying something similar to this:

If you believe God's Word, pray along with me.

*Dear Jesus, I know I am a sinner. I know that You were sent by God to die on the cross, to save me from my sins. I ask You now to forgive me of the sins I have committed, and come into my heart. Thank You for dying on the cross for me, and for rising from the dead. From this day forward, I will follow Your will and serve You. Amen.*

If you prayed that prayer, and believe, welcome to the kingdom of God!

You can help this new Christian to grow by encouraging her to find a church, get a Bible, and pray daily. For more information about how to lead someone to Christ and help them grow in their faith, visit these websites:

- www.discipleshiptools.org/
- www.matthewmcgee.org/roman-rd.html
- www.allaboutgod.com/roman-road.htm
- www.fishthe.net/digitracts/roman.htm#RomanRoad

God bless you as you carry out the life-changing work of helping guide women into relationship with Jesus Christ!

— CHAPTER TWO —

# Attending to Self-Care

## Before You Meet

### Prayer

*Lord, help me to encourage the women in my group to practice good self-care. When I share my story of self-care, use it to motivate them to begin taking first steps. If I need improvement in this area, help me to be transparent and to obey You. May we all be stirred up to take better care of ourselves spiritually, emotionally, and physically so we can better nurture those You've placed around us from a position of strength. Amen.*

### Introduction

Self-care, or the lack of it, impacts a woman in ways far greater than can be observed by the human eye. Its profit is felt on a spiritual, intellectual, and physiological level. Self-care is a gift that strengthens women from the inside out.

43

Though some women overindulge in practicing self-care, at least the physical aspects, most neglect these life-enhancing rituals and need permission to care for themselves. When women do, they nurture those they love from a position of strength that benefits her as well as those whose lives she touches.

### Discussion Preparation

Since you are a mentor, many will take your spiritual health and self-care for granted. As you prepare for this lesson, spend some extra time asking God to reveal any areas of your spiritual life that you've been neglecting. If God reveals anything to you, attend to it before you next meet to mentor others.

Jot down any of the following emotions you've recently experienced: guilt, shame, envy, anger, or fear. What was your response? If you tend to escape (books, television, Internet, busyness) or medicate (shopping, activity, eating, drinking alcohol) rather than facing the source of unwelcome emotions, admit this to your group. Recall the source of this emotion and be prepared to share. Reveal any wrong thinking that hasn't lined up with God's word.

Make a list of all the things you have done (or will do) to improve your eating habits. If living healthy hasn't been a priority in your life, read one of the books I've recommended for this chapter and come prepared to share what you've learned.

Think back to the schedule you were keeping when you were the age of the women you mentor. If you had it to do over, what would you do differently, if anything? You have the benefit of hindsight—share it with them!

Make a list in your journal of pleasurable activities that feed your well-being, as well as helpful tips for working them into your day. For instance, though I love to cook, making dinner after a hectic day can seem like just another chore. In order to make it more pleasurable, I turn on some of my favorite CDs and drink a delicious beverage. These simple actions insert a bit of self-care into a busy day, while enhancing, rather than neglecting, what needs to get done.

## When You Meet
### First Steps Accountability
Before beginning discussion on chapter 2, hold the women accountable for the First Steps listed at the end of chapter 1 (p. 38).

+ **Share** a story that resulted when you took the First Steps.
+ **Ask** the women which steps they took and encourage them to share any results with the group.

### Recap
With the demands of having grown-up responsibilities, it becomes increasingly important to practice spiritual, emotional, and physical self-care. Doing so provides peace, joy, and a sense of well-being, which in turn equips you to better handle relationship challenges.

### Points to Emphasize
Highlight the fact that unless women care for themselves spiritually, emotionally, and physically, they'll be ill-equipped to take on and sustain the exciting challenges presented in subsequent chapters.

Share any helpful advice for making time with God each day. Realizing many in your group are young moms, don't lay a guilt trip on them. I often advise young moms to meditate on one verse a day. Maybe you've found other time-efficient, yet meaningful ways to connect with God. Share them.

Encourage women in the group to share any healthy eating tips they've discovered.

Make a special point to review the facts about the benefits of getting an extra hour of sleep (p. 53).

### Loving God's Word
Encourage the women to rewrite Psalm 119:80 MSG (found on page 41) in their own words sometime during the week.

### First Steps for Next Time
Remind the women to take the First Steps on page 56 and let them know you'll be asking about their progress during your next meeting.

### Creative Touch (Optional)

At the conclusion of the lesson, offer mini-spa treatment(s) such as:

+ hot-paraffin wax to dip hands and/or feet into
+ exfoliating hand scrub and moisturizing lotion
+ facials (engage a skin-care distributor to do this for free)
+ pedicures

—————————— CHAPTER THREE ——————————

# Living as the Genuine Article

## Before You Meet

### Prayer

*Lord, I thank You that You exchange our failures for Your grace and mercy, which produce the power to live mask-free. In Jesus' name, I renounce a spirit of fear which might try to prevent these women from living in the freedom You provided by Your death on the cross. Holy Spirit, sharpen our awareness of cleverly concealed masks. During our time together, help these women glimpse the power and beauty of living authentically. In Jesus' name, amen.*

### Introduction

When the topic of living genuinely was first presented to me for possible inclusion in this book, I didn't get it. I wondered why this was an important topic for women. And then God used difficult circumstances occurring within my family to show me the disingenuous areas of my life and how they were crippling my ability to carry out the good plans He had for me.

Compare a genuine life and an authentic high-end purse. Unlike their knock-off counterparts, the genuine handbag's stitching won't come loose, the leather won't tear, the edges won't fray. Quality ingredients produce beauty in the craftsman's hands and add to his reputation.

46

A genuine life is no different. If the quality of authenticity permeates our being, we will become an object of beauty in God's hands, prepared to go the distance, bringing glory to our Maker. Hiding behind masks keeps us from experiencing intimacy with God and others. Removing masks allows us to experience fulfillment in our relationships.

### *Discussion Preparation*

Can you remember how you felt when you encountered a woman who was open and honest about her struggles in light of God's Word? Journal about how this experience impacted you.

Think about the motives that cause you to hide behind a mask. List them.

Have you seen (or worn) masks by a different name, other than those listed in the chapter? Jot them down. They may come in handy during the discussion.

## When You Meet
### *First Steps Accountability*

Before beginning discussion on chapter 3, hold the women accountable for the First Steps listed at the end of chapter 2 (p. 56).

+ **Share** a story that resulted when you took the First Steps.
+ **Ask** the women which steps they took and encourage them to share any results with the group.

### *Recap*

It is tempting to hide behind masks to keep others from seeing the real you, but the work to keep up the masquerade is exhausting, and it alters the true relationship that you could have with your husband and others. If you desire closer relationships, learn how God exposes the presence of masks and tenderly removes them. Living as the Genuine Article, you will enjoy more peace, freedom, and intimacy.

### *Points to Emphasize*

Today's young women seem not to struggle with transparency as much as women from my generation (baby boomers). However, sharing honestly is not the complete package of authentic living. Living authentically involves squaring the reality of your life with your beliefs. Your role as mentor may involve helping them shape their beliefs by holding up Scripture as a model. The more open and transparent you are in light of Scripture, the more you'll draw others to Christ.

Many young women I've talked to have a difficult time trusting other women. They're always shocked yet deeply touched when they encounter loving, godly, supportive women in Beautiful Womanhood groups. Be prepared to pray with them at the conclusion of the meeting, drawing them to forgive those who may have hurt them in the past.

Remind the women in your group about the importance of protecting things said to them in confidence.

### Loving God's Word
Read Colossians 3:12 aloud during your meeting.

### First Steps for Next Time
Read through the First Steps for chapter 3 and let the women know you will ask them if they took the steps at your next meeting.

### Creative Touch (Optional)
Gather supplies for making masquerade masks that depict an assortment of things women hide behind.

---

— CHAPTER FOUR —

## Cultivating Mystique

## Before You Meet
### Prayer
*Lord, by the power of the Holy Spirit, help me communicate Your great love to the precious women in my group that You've purchased with the blood of Your Son. Help me convey the knowl-*

*edge that You've got great plans for each individual woman—no matter her past or present. Help these women to believe that they are a unique expression of God's creativity and that each is beautiful in His sight. Fill them with courage to express their unique beauty. As they grow in confidence, may they focus more on others than on themselves so they can minister to their family and those hurting people You bring across their path. In Jesus' name, amen.*

### Introduction

At the age of forty-five, I finally realized (through difficulty) that I had misconceptions about God's love for me that were hindering my confidence in areas of worth, position, personality, and relationships. These misconceptions were created by looking to people and events to define me while ascribing their interpretations to God. Any time we make people bigger than God we've bowed our knee to a false god and unwittingly participated in Satan's plans for us. Believing God's thoughts about you will have a positive domino effect in the way you live your life and choose to express yourself. It also improves your relationship with your husband and enables you to fulfill the good plans God has for your life.

### Discussion Preparation

One of the greatest deficits in a woman's life is inner confidence, so it's critical you share the steps you've taken to cultivate and grow mystique. A lack of confidence affects all areas of a woman's life. Without it, her relationships will be negatively impacted (as mine were), she'll be prevented from fulfilling the good plans God designed for her to complete, and she'll miss out on the freedom and joy that comes from expressing her unique personality and godly attitudes.

Sharing your own journey toward assurance is the most important thing you'll talk about this week. Without an understanding of your tremendous worth to Christ, *advancement* and *appearance* are just fluff and nonsense and your *attitudes* won't be motivated by love. When a woman has a confident belief in her worth, position, personality, and relationships, she will be a powerful tool in God's hands to draw others to Himself.

Before the lesson, look up Scripture verses relating to gossip. This may be an issue that women in your group struggle with, so it is good to come ready with God's truth on the topic.

The topic of appearance might not be your strong suit—but stay with me now, because it can be a lot of fun. You're never too old to cultivate this aspect of your mystique! Here are some helpful hints for beginning to define your style:

+ List famous women whose fashion sense you admire. This will help you develop a language that defines your mystique and will aid you in purchasing clothes (e.g., Grace Kelly—Vintage Elegance; Anne Hathaway—Modern Sophistication; Carrie Underwood—Country Chic).
+ Determine which retail stores offer fashions you like. Either through their advertisements, or by asking in person, find out how they define the style their clothing line represents.
+ Ask a stylish friend for help.
+ Employ the help of a personal stylist (they can be affordable—do an online search for personal stylists in your city). Any stylist worth her salt won't make you over into something you're not. She'll help unveil the best you.

If you haven't before, what better time could there be to define your mystique and express your unique, God-given personality from the inside out? The women in your group will benefit from your example.

## When You Meet
### First Steps Accountability
Before beginning discussion on chapter 4, hold the women accountable for the First Steps listed at the end of chapter 3 (p. 69).

+ **Share** a story that resulted when you took the First Steps.
+ **Ask** the women which steps they took and encourage them to share any results with the group.

### Recap

"Why try so hard to fit in when you were born to stand out?" Growing in your mystique increases your peace and confidence and improves your relationship with your husband and others. You can build your inner confidence through an assurance of God's love, advancing in your passions, improving your appearance, and developing godly attitudes.

### Points to Emphasize

+ Discovering one's personal style is not an excuse for abusing the budget and ultimately should save time and money.
+ When discussing attitudes, it's important to make this connection: Knowing and experiencing God's love = increased confidence = good attitudes = improved relationships.
+ Encourage the women to ask God to show them areas of their husband's life where he needs encouragement. Ask them to start a list of God's promises so they can refresh their husbands with God's Word when needed.
+ Talking about mystique is fun *and* challenging. Remind the women mystique is not cultivated in a day, and it's not something that they arrive at and then they're done! It's a lifelong journey. After reading the chapter, spend time in prayer asking God to help you communicate His unconditional love and your personal cultivation of mystique to the women in your group.

### Loving God's Word

Write out Ephesians 2:10, inserting your name in the passage and place it where it will remind you of your worth daily. Encourage group members to do the same.

### First Steps for Next Time

Remind the women to take the First Steps on page 87 and tell them you will hold them accountable for taking these steps at your next group meeting. The completion of first steps is very important. If they know you'll ask, they'll be more likely to follow through.

### Creative Touch (Optional)
+ Plan a field trip to a makeup counter at the mall to learn about application techniques or the correct colors for each woman's skin tone.
+ Ask a personal stylist or makeup artist to come to your home to conduct a "makeover" for someone in the group.

### Creative Touch in Preparation for Chapter 5 (Optional)
After discussing chapter 4, ask the women to bring a wedding photo to the next meeting.

--- CHAPTER FIVE ---

# Inviting Romance

## Before You Meet
### Prayer
*Dear Lord, as I think about the steps to inviting romance, I'm painfully aware of my own shortcomings in this area. Use my honesty to encourage others in the group. Help me to encourage the women by conveying an excitement about doing things differently—according to Your Word—in order to increase romance. Heighten my sensitivity to women who may not have caused the lack of romance and intimacy in their marriage. If abuse is occurring in the life of any woman in my group, reveal it by the power of the Holy Spirit. Give me the courage I'll need to lead her to safety. In Jesus' name, amen.*

### Introduction
The desire for romance and intimacy beats strong within the hearts of women, but how do you reach this state of warmth and

connectedness with your husband? Movies, television, and romance novels don't offer any practical suggestions that work for godly women living in the real world. But God does. Within Scripture, we find principles that work for experiencing romance in marriage.

When you
>  **T**rust instead of control
>  **R**espect instead of demean
>  **A**ppreciate instead of criticize
>  **C**onfer confidence instead of doubt
>  **E**xpose vulnerability instead of defensiveness

you **TRACE** a path to more romance.

### Discussion Preparation

As you read "Inviting Romance," did you feel a pang of regret remembering a time when your words and actions may have doused the romance in your marriage? The temptation to control, disrespect, doubt, and defend runs deep within most women.

God wants to help us escape temptations like these. "The temptations that come into your life are no different from what others experience. And God is faithful. He will keep the temptation from becoming so strong that you can't stand up against it. When you are tempted, he will show you a way out so that you will not give in to it" (1 Corinthians 10:13). Pause, turn to God, and ask Him to show you a new way of doing things. Thankfully, we can also encourage one another to resist these romance-dousing tendencies.

When I was leading a Beautiful Womanhood small group on the topic of Inviting Romance, one woman came under strong conviction from the Holy Spirit concerning the disrespect she had consistently shown her husband. She began to cry, realizing with fresh awareness the pain she must have caused him during a recent episode. As I laid my hand on her arm, I asked her what she might do to show respect in the situation she had shared. She came up with several steps she could take and the group cheered her on while sharing their own journeys. This woman could hardly wait to leave my home and make amends. She was well on her way to inviting romance into her marriage!

If you're a mentor with a laid-back disposition who doesn't really struggle with the issues discussed in this chapter, ask God to give you compassion for those who do struggle with the five steps to romance. When you're leading the discussion, make mention of personality differences that affect these behaviors and remind them you struggle in other areas.

## When You Meet
### First Steps Accountability
Before beginning discussion on chapter 5, hold the women accountable for the First Steps listed at the end of chapter 4 (p. 87).

+ **Share** a story that resulted when you took the First Steps.
+ **Ask** the women which steps they took and encourage them to share any results with the group.

### Recap
Most women dream of romance, but many don't consider whether their words and actions are stumbling blocks or invitations to their husband to join them in a romantic relationship. The saying, "If you do what you've always done, you'll get what you've always gotten" rings true in regard to romance. Reflect a moment on the results of your actions and words and ask, "Do I like what I'm getting?" If not, you can trace a new path to romance. To help you take these new steps, remember the acronym TRACE—Trust, Respect, Appreciate, Confer Confidence, and Expose Vulnerability.

### Points to Emphasize
In the section Trust Instead of Control, point out the difference between advising your husband when he's asked you for help and doing so unasked. The latter exhibits a controlling nature, which inhibits romance. When a wife is asked for input, she should respond thoughtfully, with biblical wisdom. If it would help her to choose the right words and the right tone, she can ask her husband to let her think about it a bit before she answers.

Before discussing the fifth step to romance—Expose Vulnerability Instead of Defensiveness—make certain to mention exceptions in the case of emotionally or physically abusive relationships. A mentor must *never assume* the lack of abuse in the marriages represented within her group. Statistics prove that one out of every four women are abused either emotionally, physically, or spiritually—and these reflect only the cases reported. Most abused women protect their husbands at all cost so abuse can be difficult to detect at a surface level. Abused women will suffer more if they expose vulnerability to their husbands. Sadly, most abused women are constantly assessing their own behavior with the hope of improving the relationship. It never works.

If a woman begins sharing stories that indicate abuse, your first response should be to tell her it's not her fault. Make sure your face reflects love and concern, and offer to pray with her. Tell her you want to connect her with someone who can help. Either contact a pastor at your church and ask to be referred to a reputable Christian counselor, or call the Domestic Abuse Hotline at 1-800-799-SAFE.

### Loving God's Word

Read Isaiah 30:15 and lead a discussion about how your group might apply it to their life and marriage.

### First Steps for Next Time

Remind the women to take the First Steps on page 105 and tell them you will hold them accountable at your next group meeting. The completion of First Steps is very important. If they know you'll ask, they'll be more likely to follow through.

### Creative Touch (Optional)

Ask each woman to show her wedding photo and share what first attracted her to her husband.

# CHAPTER SIX

# Thinking Differently About Sex

## Before You Meet
### Prayer

*Lord, prepare me to lead this discussion about the wonder and mystery of sex. Where I still struggle with issues myself, touch me with Your healing power and strengthen me to make better choices. Encourage me to share my struggles for the good of the group. Equip me to answer the tough questions, and when I don't have answers, help me to point women in the direction of someone who can. Enfold me in Your arms of love so that I can give from the overflow to a woman who's been hurting for a long time. May every part of me exude Your love and compassion for them. Help me to grasp and convey the importance of changing the way we think about sex so we can experience a little of heaven here on earth with our husbands. Heal and help us in Jesus' name! Amen.*

### Introduction

Sex is a subject that has affected my life and marriage like few other things—and I'm not alone. It's one of the top three issues couples fight about. Sexual abuse, date rape, premarital sex, infidelity, and pornography have wounded many women, and few have successfully found resolution for the emotional pain and destruction these abuses create. Thus, it impacts marriage greatly. For this reason, it's important we talk about sex.

Thought precedes action. Changing the way the women in your group think about sex enables them to throw a switch in their brain. This switch holds the potential to enhance their sex life. Sex provides wonderful benefits and fulfills vital needs within marriage.

It's been my experience that women want to understand what God has to say about sex. Living in a highly sexualized culture, they find it difficult to distinguish between growing into an exciting lover and staying free from cultural pressures. Women can encourage each other by talking about sex.

### *Discussion Preparation*

If you're uncomfortable talking about sex, spend time in prayer asking God why. Ask Him to free you from unnatural inhibitions so you can minister grace and truth to the women in your group. They need to hear from godly women about sex! God created sex, and we should not be ashamed to talk about it—so don't be shy. To prepare to lead the discussion, take time to journal your responses to the following prompts:

+ Think back over your sexual journey, and make note of the bumps you've hit. Be prepared to discuss these as well as any painful issues that have affected your sex life. If you haven't dealt with these issues, ask yourself how it's affected your sex life and be ready to share some candid reflections with the women in your group. Your story may serve as the catalyst for another woman to get the help she needs.
+ If you've got an active sex life, think about how you've successfully prioritized this important aspect of marriage. If you're living life at the pace of a NASCAR race, be prepared to share how this has affected your sex life.
+ Think about how you've seduced your husband through the years and share your ideas with the women in your group. We can all benefit from creative inspiration.

The women in your group will have varied experiences and, sadly, many of the women you mentor will have had a negative experience with sex. So for this discussion, it's good to be prepared for the painful incidents that may be revealed.

Don't fear these revelations; instead, welcome them! One of my prayers for Beautiful Womanhood small groups is that women will have the opportunity to divulge their painful past in a safe, loving community of women. Sexual wounds are often exposed when other negative life experiences are erupting. It's as if dynamite is needed to dislodge dark secrets buried deep within the heart. Preferably, women will have the opportunity to deal with their past without the complication of simultaneous negative circumstances.

In a sexual abuse recovery workbook, *The Journey Begins*, produced by Open Hearts Ministries, we find wise guidance for how to respond when someone shares their journey: "How we respond to another person's story is important. When a person decides the group is a safe place to reveal his or her story, we must consider it a gift, one that is given tentatively. Years of silence, harmful responses [or] a fear of being responsible . . . keep[s] stories buried."

God has given us a picture in His Word of how to respond to feeling exposed. When Adam and Eve felt shame for the first time, they realized they were naked, became afraid, and hid. And "the Lord God made clothing from animal skins for Adam and his wife (Genesis 3:21). God clothed them, covering their shame with grace and truth.

If a woman reveals a deeply painful past experience, be prepared to help "re-clothe" her by your response. Here are some helpful suggestions:

- Let the woman know how you feel about what happened to her. Use words that feel like a warm embrace to let her know she is not alone with her pain and hurt. ("I'm so sorry you had to endure that painful treatment.")
- Move toward a woman in shame with your words. ("I value what you shared with us. Your story is worth hearing.")
- Maintain open body language—open posture, don't back away or cross your arms.
- Express your compassion with your face. Allow your tears to flow, give plenty of eye contact, and don't look angry or shocked.

## When You Meet
### *First Steps Accountability*
Before beginning discussion on chapter 6, hold the women accountable for the First Steps listed at the end of chapter 5 (p. 105).

+ **Share** a story that resulted when you took the First Steps.
+ **Ask** the women which steps they took and encourage them to share any results with the group.

### *Recap*

You have the power to change the way you think about sex by replacing old thoughts with new ones. Understanding God's purposes for sex, your husband's deep emotional need for sex, and how you view yourself as a sexual woman alters your thought life, which in turn benefits your sex life. No matter what your past, God desires for sex in your marriage to be a blessing to both you and your husband.

### *Points to Emphasize*

Highlight a husband's need to connect with his wife on a deep emotional level and reiterate that sex is his point of connection. Remind the women that, often, sex holds the key to the intimacy we desire.

Underscore how sex with a fully engaged wife makes a husband feel loved, desired, and confident (p. 113). Explore how this would transform your husband and bless you.

You may be asked if certain activities in and outside the bedroom are acceptable. I often am. A woman in one Beautiful Womanhood group told me her husband asked her to go braless in public and then asked me what I thought about it. I told her that going braless can cause other men to lust and that we are held accountable for our actions. On the other hand, I'm not against bralessness at home! It's important to seduce your husband with what you wear or don't wear. I recommended she spice her bedroom wardrobe up a bit to show him she wasn't against having fun. Kevin Leman's book, *Sheet Music*, tastefully addresses some of these sensitive topics in light of Scripture. Pick up a copy of his book so you're prepared.

Some of the women in your group may be married to men who are disinterested in sex for one of many reasons. *Intimate Issues*, which is listed in the recommended reading section of *The Beautiful Wife*, includes a chapter entitled, "What Do I Do When HE Has a Headache?" Before you meet with your group, buy or borrow the book and read the chapter. Many of the women I encounter are struggling as a result of this issue and you should be prepared.

### Loving God's Word

Focus your prayer time around Ephesians 5:31–32.

### First Steps for Next Time

Read through the First Steps for chapter 6 and let the women know you will ask them if they took the steps at your next meeting.

### Creative Touch (Optional)

Make romantic (suggestive?) notes together to stick in a husband's lunch box or on his pillow or at his computer—anywhere he's likely to find them. Encourage women to spritz them with his favorite perfume or add a lipsticked kiss. Go crazy and make one for each day of the upcoming week, but be prepared for the results!

—————— CHAPTER SEVEN ——————

# Opening Lines of Communication

## Before You Meet
### Prayer

*Lord, help me to be an understanding wife! Come assist me as I share with my group the importance of resolving issues in a loving, effective manner that doesn't confuse or threaten their husbands. Please give them an awareness of wrong thought patterns that have hindered communication in the past so they can make better choices. They need your strength and courage for this, Lord. Please give them a "Pam Farrel garage story" of their own to encourage them on this path. If they need it, guide them to seek additional help from books or counselors to improve their communication skills. Give their husbands an understanding wife. In Jesus' name, amen.*

### Introduction

Good communication is difficult to achieve as attested by the fact it's one of the top three issues couples deal with. In a recent Beautiful Womanhood survey, women indicated that they desire help with communication in marriage above all other topics. Keeping the lines of communication open takes practice and commitment, but the rewards of greater understanding are well worth it.

### Discussion Preparation

Though I touch on a few components of good communication that were absent from Tom's and my communication breakdown, there are several more tools that the women in your group should be aware of. Review this list and journal about some examples from your marriage so you are ready to share with the group:

- Escalation, negative interpretations, and pursuing and withdrawing are further patterns that destroy oneness and prevent understanding between a man and his wife. It would be useful for you to understand a few of these concepts before beginning the discussion. In *A Lasting Promise* by Scott Stanley, you will find these ideas explained. It's one of the best books on communication Tom and I have read.
- Effective communication skills consist of speaking directly, kindly, and at the proper place and time. This increases your chances of being understood.
- Effective listening skills require controlling your tongue and listening with an ear to understand your husband's ideas and feelings. This increases the probability that your husband will feel understood, thus opening lines of communication.

Take time to journal about an instance of communication breakdown in your marriage. Be sure to convey how not being understood made you or your husband feel. This will reinforce the need to grow in this area. Make sure to include which points of good communication you neglected: being direct, kindness, choosing the proper time and place, listening, or any other techniques or principles you've learned about. Be prepared to share this story at the start of the group discussion.

## When You Meet
### First Steps Accountability

Before beginning discussion on chapter 7, hold the women accountable for the First Steps listed at the end of chapter 6 (p. 124).

+ **Share** a story that resulted when you took the First Steps.
+ **Ask** the women which steps they took and encourage them to share any results with the group.

### Recap

A lack of good communication skills causes hurt, loneliness, and isolation. Understanding root causes of ineffective communication will help you reverse negative patterns and increase your ability to paint a clear picture with your words—one that a man is more likely to see and understand.

### Points to Emphasize

After opening with prayer, begin by sharing your story about a communication breakdown that happened in your marriage.

It may be helpful to read aloud the story I shared from Pam Farrel (*The Beautiful Wife*, pp. 135–36). I get chills every time I read it! Most women can relate to a lack of interest in something their husband finds interesting enough to talk about. Mustering attentiveness (if only repeating back what he says) holds the potential to unlock the intimacy we desire.

When first attempting mirroring with my husband, I didn't even listen well to my counselor (OK, I had a big problem) because I thought I was supposed to take Tom's words and put them into my words. My natural instinct was to interpret rather than use *his* words. You may need to underscore this point.

Validation was and is also difficult for me. Remind the women that validation doesn't require that you agree with what the other person is saying. You don't have to like it either! The object is to confirm what your husband said and begin to see the issue from *his* perspective. Ask God for help seeing your husband's perspective.

An important point to stress about empathy is this: let go of your own viewpoint for a few moments and see the issue from his angle, feeling what he feels. If this reminds you of a story, be prepared to share it.

Do you resolve issues or do they linger to surface another day? Tom and I still deal with unresolved issues that erupted in the past that afflict our relationship with pain. Emphasize the need to deal with issues as they arise without backing their husbands into a corner.

### Loving God's Word

Encourage the women to read and reflect on Ecclesiastes 3:7.

### First Steps for Next Time

Read through the First Steps at the end of chapter 7 and let the women know you will ask them if they took the steps at your next meeting.

### Creative Touch (Optional)

Download a video about communication by Emerson Eggerichs from YouTube or the Love and Respect website (www.loveandrespect .com). Watch it during your meeting.

---------------- CHAPTER EIGHT ----------------

## Speaking Truth in Love

## Before You Meet
### Prayer

*Lord, prepare me in every way needed to share this lesson. I know that women today face difficult issues within marriage, as I have. Help the passive women be brave and courageous as they read this chapter. Remind the bold to put on meekness—strength under control. May each woman exchange her pain for Your love. May she give her burdens to You, Lord, so You can care for her. Do not permit any of these women to slip and fall. Have Your way in each of their lives so that they or their husbands will turn from wickedness and be healed. Amen.*

## Introduction

We all encounter others' sinful behavior at one time or another. Sadly, many people disregard God's instruction for dealing with sin because it can be difficult to confront someone.

Because God loves all His children, He's counting on us to help carry out His redemptive plan in the world. He chooses to use us. What a God! What a relationship! What purpose!

How can we deny His request to help lift His son or daughter up from their pit of bad choices? If more people responded to God by speaking truth in love, the world would certainly look different. Join Him in this redemptive work. When we find ourselves faced with bad or evil situations and choose to speak the truth in love, we become more and more like Christ in every way.

Most likely everyone in your Beautiful Womanhood group, including you, knows someone who's in a bad place and needs to hear the truth spoken in love. Encouraging the women to employ what they learn could be critical to someone lost in sin and will bless the woman herself.

## Discussion Preparation

Before you meet as a group, prepare a list of Christian counselors (include contact information) for a woman who reveals a desperate situation that requires help beyond what you can offer. Assure her she is not alone as the group will be supporting her in prayer.

## When You Meet
### First Steps Accountability

Before beginning discussion on chapter 8, hold the women accountable for First Steps listed at the end of chapter 7 (p. 139).

+ **Share** a story that resulted when you took the First Steps.
+ **Ask** the women which steps they took and encourage them to share any results with the group.

### *Recap*

Are you struggling with your husband's sinful behavior? Before you speak assertively, two things are required: an honest examination of the truth about your behavior as well as your husband's, and a liberal application of love to your words.

### *Points to Emphasize*

Discuss the struggle between determining if a behavior in question is sinful or annoying. Remember, if you regularly use your influence to spotlight annoyances, you'll have little influence left to deal with sin.

Reinforce The Truth About You section (p. 144), as this is the essence of becoming a beautiful wife. Before speaking to her husband, a woman must examine her own actions in the light of God's Word. If you meet with complaints of unfairness, remind the women that the person making the first move toward healing demonstrates greater maturity.

Speaking truth in love requires a choice and preparation. You must *choose* to love someone enough to make the effort of *preparation* before you speak to them. Some people may be able to speak loving truth on the fly, but most (including me) cannot. Recommend that the women journal about the situation first, dividing their writing into sections of truth, love, and speaking. Encourage them to pray for the person they'll speak to and ask God to show them the proper place and time to communicate. (If women are using *The Beautiful Wife Prayer Journal*, this process is prompted on page 54.)

A word about forgiveness: If a woman has been wounded by her husband's sin, gently remind her that forgiveness is essential for her well-being. When you choose to hold grudges, you wound yourself. If your husband asks for forgiveness, give it freely. If he doesn't, forgive him before God. Don't tell your husband you forgive him if he hasn't confessed his sin, but forgive him in prayer before God. Let the Holy Spirit do the work of conviction in his heart, not you.

### Loving God's Word

Memorize Ephesians 4:15: "Instead, we will hold to the truth in love, becoming more and more in every way like Christ." Encourage the women in your group to memorize this with you.

### First Steps for Next Time

Remind the women to take the First Steps on page 161 and let them know you'll be asking about their progress during your next meeting.

### Creative Touch (Optional)

Write out hypothetical scenarios where speaking assertively is needed for clear communication. Place them in a bowl and let each woman select one. Using the skills learned about assertive speaking, take turns practicing.

Examples:

+ Your husband asks you to run an important errand for him in the middle of a jam-packed day and you have *no* time available in your schedule.
+ A friend begins gossiping about someone in your church.
+ You find pornography on your husband's computer.

———————————————— CHAPTER NINE ————————————————

# Managing Money

## Before You Meet
### Prayer

*Lord, I thank you for all You've revealed in Your Word about money. Please use my history with money (whether good or bad) to encourage the women I mentor. Help me to convey the principles held in Your Word in a compelling way so women will be motivated to follow them. I pray the women will use discretion when sharing the things they've learned with their husbands. Help them to be wise in their approach and to rely on You to motivate their husband's response. Give them courage to change negative spending habits they see in themselves, and even greater courage if they see them in their husband. I pray that You will radically fill us all with a strong desire to become wise managers of the money You entrust to us. In Jesus' name, amen.*

### Introduction

Today, many families are suffering from the economy's downturn and heavy debt loads, so sharing biblical insights about money is a timely topic. Additionally, those who are prospering need to hear this message because organizations doing good work around the world in the name of Christ are in desperate need of funds to carry out their God-given mission.

Money is an exceedingly spiritual topic, and in my experience, it hasn't been given nearly enough "press" in the church. I'm thrilled to include this chapter in *The Beautiful Wife* so women have a chance to discuss and come to a better understanding about the topic written about over two thousand times in the Bible—topping the number of verses written about prayer and faith combined.

Understanding God's financial plan and getting on the same page with your husband will ease stress and tension in your marriage and allow you to more easily meet the needs of others.

### Discussion Preparation

As you prepare for this lesson, look back into your past to discover any self-defeating, negative messages you may have received about money. Reflect on how these affected you, your finances, and your marriage.

If you and your husband are not tithers and you're intrigued by the thought of putting God to the test, journal a commitment to trying it, and share this with the women in your group along with the results of your test. There's no time like the present to follow God in all aspects of your life.

If you and your husband are living by a financial plan, think about how this came to be and why. If you are managing your finances using a spending plan, reflect on how this has affected you. Journal some thoughts. Come to the lesson prepared to share honestly how the plan—or the lack of a plan—has affected your finances and how you're managing with God's help.

Think about how you determined who would handle the finances in your marriage—you or your husband—and whether or not this choice affected your finances or marriage for good or bad. Journal some reflections.

## When You Meet
### First Steps Accountability
Before beginning discussion on chapter 9, hold the women accountable for the First Steps listed at the end of chapter 8 (p. 161).

+ **Share** a story that resulted when you took the First Steps.
+ **Ask** the women which steps they took and encourage them to share any results with the group.

### Recap
There is a financial plan that leads to peace in your life and harmony in your marriage. In this chapter, you'll discover how adjusting your financial attitude, recognizing God's ownership, and getting on the same financial page with your husband can bring the true financial freedom that comes from God.

### Points to Emphasize
Many Christians have little knowledge of the important biblical principle of stewardship. Review Matthew 25:14–30 in light of Randy Alcorn's analogy (p. 165) in order to explain the concept of steward or money manager.

Tithing is another concept that needs emphasis in our day. Review Malachi 3:10, the biblical basis for percentage giving and priority giving (pp. 166–67).

### Loving God's Word

Before starting the discussion of chapter 9, "Managing Money," read 1 Timothy 6:10 aloud to the group.

### First Steps for Next Time

Remind the women to take First Steps on page 180 and tell them you will hold them accountable for taking these steps at your next group meeting. Accountability produces a greater likelihood of change.

### Creative Touch (Optional)

Find a YouTube video from Randy Alcorn, Dave Ramsey, or another financial expert you trust. Watch it together as a group.

———————————— CHAPTER TEN ————————————

# Creating a Culture of Beauty

## Before You Meet

### Prayer

*Lord, thank You for sharing Your love of beauty with me and giving me Your creative ability to express it. As I teach this lesson, give me the words I need to share how vital it is to create a culture of beauty at home. Help me to convey the importance of maintaining a steady emotional barometer in the home and to encourage the women to turn to You for help with their issues and problems. As I stand in support of family mealtime, illumine the group's understanding of its great value and give them strength to go against the grain of society to make it happen. I pray You would spark a desire in them to welcome lost and lonely*

*people into their homes and offer them relief from life's storms.
In Jesus' name, amen.*

### Introduction

When my husband and I had the privilege of traveling to Europe, we became witnesses to a culture of beauty I had never before experienced. Opposed to seeing the world from a tour bus, we spent our time in small towns living among the locals. Special memories from the trip include cozy down comforters, waiters devoted to a lengthy dining experience (they shun the idea of rushing diners to make way for new customers), delicious food served simply yet beautifully, colorful flowers on display indoors and out, and non-hurried people who take time to talk and play with one another. Experiencing this tangible and relational beauty changed the way I live my life in America because it made such a lasting impact on me.

You can create an energizing culture of beauty like this within your home by demonstrating your personal expression of beauty, adopting right attitudes, and focusing on your relationships with your husband and children. When a woman is focused on creating a culture of beauty, her family and friends, new and old, will relish the hours spent in her home and will be changed because of them.

I've recently felt the tug of the Holy Spirit to invite fellow churchgoers into our home after service. We attend a large seeker-friendly church, so experiencing intimacy is almost impossible. I'm challenged to pray and then ask someone sitting close by if they'd like to join us for a meal in our home. I'm excited about the possibilities. To what lengths would God go to place hurting, needy people close by Tom and me if He knew we were making ourselves available to show them hospitality and care? Look around, the harvest is ripe for the picking with so many hurting, needy people.

### Discussion Preparation

If you are hosting the small group in your home, it can be fun to lead by example on the topic of creating a culture of beauty, but be careful you don't overdo it. One Beautiful Womanhood mentor shared with me that she was excited to share beauty with the women in her group. She invested much effort in sending beautifully decorated invitations, setting a beautiful table, and creating a beautiful atmosphere in general. At the conclusion of twelve lessons, when the mentor suggested getting together regularly at each other's homes for further accountability and fellowship, no one volunteered. Looking back, she realized that although the women were excited to meet together and discuss each lesson, they were intimidated by all the finishing touches she had lovingly created—she had overdone a good thing.

Hospitality seems to have become a lost art. It is something we are encouraged to do throughout Scripture, yet many Christians overlook this amazing opportunity to share Christ's love. By discussing this chapter, you're presented with a prime opportunity to exert your influence by encouraging hospitality in the homes of the women you mentor. As a woman who is modeling hospitality by investing in their lives, you can cheer them on to do the same.

### First Steps Accountability

Before beginning discussion on chapter 10, hold the women accountable for First Steps listed at the end of chapter 9 (p. 180).

+ **Share** a story that resulted when you took the First Steps.
+ **Ask** the women which steps they took and encourage them to share any results with the group.

### Recap

Beauty is energy creating. You can bless your husband, children, and all those who visit by creating beauty in your home. God has given you a unique expression of beauty, and your home can reflect your individuality—even on a tight budget. You can also express the beauty of your spirit by pursuing peace, cultivating contentment, and being slow to anger as you focus your time and attention on your husband, children, and extending warm hospitality to others.

### Points to Emphasize

In a culture obsessed with materialism, it will be important in your discussion to strike the balance between creating beauty in your home and doing it within a budget you and your husband agree on. When my husband and I added on a great room to our old farmhouse, he was making a good income and we failed to set a budget. Between the two of us, we came up with amazing ideas and implemented most. Sadly, we overspent to the degree that we may not ever recoup the money we invested. I created an imbalance between expressing my personal style and stewarding God's money faithfully.

Using every statistic you can find (do online research about the benefits of family mealtime), encourage women to prioritize or reinstate the family dinner hour. (Dare I say *hour*?) They may have to go against the grain of society to make this happen, but urge them to do so.

Women experience many effects both internal and external that cause their emotional barometers to rise and plunge. Rather than going along for the ride, it's important to evaluate the cause(s). Encourage the women to reflect on the emotional barometer in their home. If it's difficult to determine the cause of erratic, unruly emotions, suggest that they invite godly friends to speak into their life. Friends can see issues that aren't so obvious to the one afflicted and vice versa.

Invite the women to share the list of their husband's positive qualities. Because it's so much easier to focus on what irritates us than on what pleases us, remind them to read the list when struggling with the urge to complain about his aggravating tendencies.

Ask the women to think about who they know that could benefit from their hospitality. Encourage them to list them and make a plan to invite them one by one.

### Loving God's Word

Insert your name into Proverbs 31:27 and read it aloud. Encourage the women in your group to do the same.

### First Steps for Next Time

Read through the First Steps at the end of chapter 10 and let the women know you will ask them which they took at your next meeting.

### Creative Touch (Optional)

Work as a group to plan a meal for a group of people in need of the warmth hospitality provides (perhaps a few single mothers) and invite them into one of your homes. Brainstorm creative ways to express God's love to them. For instance, the group could create a party favor to send home with each guest. Consider employing a couple of husbands to serve the meal. Offer free child care at another group member's home and provide a meal, Bible story, and games for the kids to enjoy.

---

CHAPTER ELEVEN

# Professionalizing the Roles of Wife and Mother

## Before You Meet

### Prayer

*Dear Lord, as I ask You to give me a vision for my role as a wife and for my children, I pray You will fill me with excitement at the revelation! Strengthen me with Your Spirit's power to fulfill this vision. Help me to transmit the necessity of taking our roles as wives and mothers seriously. I ask You to heal me from any hurts I have harbored when my husband didn't seem to notice all I do for our family. I confess the times that I was responsible for the lack of unity between my husband and me. Help us to grow in unity, remembering it's never too late to experience its blessings. Bless and keep my children and help me to share all I'm learning—not teaching them (if they're adults), but rather sharing my story and living it out before them. May our family fulfill all the plans You have for us. In Jesus' name, amen.*

### Introduction

It's critical to the strength of our marriage and family to purposefully invest ourselves in the lives of our husbands and children—for their sakes as well as our own. To do your best in this career, talk to your Boss, determine your vision, plan action steps, get an education, and identify a mentor.

### Discussion Preparation

Before you meet with your group, take the time to determine and write down a vision for your role as wife and for your children. Develop a plan of action to see these visions through. Determine if you need an education to successfully carry out your plan of action. And, lastly, establish who your mentors are and whether or not you need their help to get you where you want to go. Record everything in your prayer journal. Going through this process yourself will help you inspire the women you mentor to do the same and allow you to relate to some of the struggles they may go through while doing so.

Unity between parents is an important theme in this chapter. Without unity, you won't experience the fullness of blessing God has for you. Recall how you and your husband have arrived at a place of unity regarding important (and not-so-important) decisions and be ready to pass these helps along.

## When You Meet

### First Steps Accountability

Before beginning discussion on chapter 11, hold the women accountable for the First Steps listed at the end of chapter 10 (p. 196).

+ **Share** a story that resulted when you took the First Steps.
+ **Ask** the women which steps they took and encourage them to share any results with the group.

### Recap

As a wife and mother, you are employed in a very important career. To do your best in this career, talk to your Boss, determine your vision, plan action steps, get an education, and identify a mentor.

### Points to Emphasize

The purpose of this chapter is not to promote an agenda that says women should stay home rather than working outside the home. Rather, its purpose is to bestow value, or, in other words, to "professionalize" the roles wives and mothers hold. Make sure this message is clear so as not to inadvertently condemn anyone in the group.

Emphasize the importance of writing down our vision. Vision keeps you from a life of self-defeat—wandering around in circles and never getting where you want to go. Journaling these steps marks out a straight path for your feet. Without a clear roadmap, you'll never reach your destination. Encourage the women to revisit their plans in a year's time. As marriage evolves and children grow, there often arises a need to tweak the plan of action.

Stress the importance of thinking about the end-game. Ask them: "If you knew there was a path that would lead you to all the good things God has for your marriage and your family, would you take it?" When they answer "yes," remind them that when they ask their Boss (God) for a good plan (vision) for their family and then listen for His instruction (plan of action), they will be pleasantly surprised by where they find themselves in a year. One of my favorite quotes by Henry David Thoreau illustrates this point, and it's posted on a corkboard in my office where it inspires me: "If one advances confidently in the direction of his dreams, and endeavors to live the life which he has imagined, he will meet with a success unexpected in common hours."

When talking about instilling good things in the lives of children, emphasize the necessity of women possessing these qualities themselves. The saying, "You can't give what you don't possess" applies here. Investing in *Mom's* education will produce good things in the lives of her children—no matter how old.

### Loving God's Word

At the conclusion of the meeting, pray a prayer of blessing over each woman using Proverbs 31:28–29. Personalize the prayer by inserting the woman's name in the blank.

*May _____'s children stand and bless her. May her husband praise her saying there are many virtuous and capable women in the world, but she surpasses them all!*

If you're comfortable doing so, lay your hand upon each woman's head while blessing them.

### First Steps for Next Time

Read through the First Steps for chapter 11 and let the women know you will ask them if they took the steps at your next meeting.

### Creative Touch (Optional)

Provide two sheets of beautiful stationery for each woman in your group. At the top of the first sheet, type or write, "Vision for My Marriage." At the top of the second, type or write, "Vision for Our Children." Encourage the women to write out their vision, frame it, and hang it in a visible location.

---

CHAPTER TWELVE

# Choosing God's Best

## Before You Meet
### Prayer

*Lord, thank You for giving me the awesome privilege of mentoring this group of beautiful women. I've experienced highs and lows, but through it all, You've been faithful to me. During this last lesson, help me to effectively emphasize the importance to choose God's best in making their marriage a priority, lest the choice be made for them by virtue of default. Provide all of them with godly mentors and accountability partners who will help cheer them on their journey. Let me know if this group should continue meeting together. Is there a purpose for us yet to be fulfilled? If so, lead and guide me on this path. Encourage me to continue mentoring wives so they can experience Your love, purpose, and hope. In Jesus' name, amen.*

### Introduction

This is an important lesson not to be taken lightly or omitted altogether. I know it's a short chapter and you may be tempted to finish early but "Choosing God's Best" deserves attention because it's a final call to action. This is where the rubber of all we've learned meets the road.

Where will you journey first? Need a little more romance, financial security, improved communication, or a more satisfying sex life? You choose! You must choose what kind of marriage you want, or you choose by default. God's best for your marriage lies within the boundaries of humility-inspired obedience.

### Discussion Preparation

Think about which chapter represented an area in which you desire more growth. Write it down. Look back in your journal and re-read what you've written in the chapter you're going to focus on. Write down what steps you'll take to experience more of God's best in your marriage. Be prepared to share this with the group.

## When You Meet
### First Steps Accountability

Before beginning discussion on chapter 12, hold the women accountable for First Steps listed at the end of chapter 11 (p. 215).

+ **Share** a story that resulted when you took the First Steps.
+ **Ask** the women which steps they took and encourage them to share any results with the group.

### Points to Emphasize

The world is quick to proclaim that you don't have to choose. "You can have it all!" The truth is, you can't. If you don't choose God's best, you won't get it. Learning how to choose God's best through humility and obedience will bring you to a place of fulfillment.

### Points to Emphasize

As you conclude chapter 12, stress the importance to *choose* to make marriage a priority. This doesn't come naturally. One of the reasons I inserted "Professionalizing the Roles of Wife and Mother" at the end of the book (chapter 11) was that women often choose to prioritize children before husbands. I understand that temptation. Children begin their lives dependent on us and later are vying for all the attention we'll give them. The needs of our marriage aren't always so obvious but that doesn't mean we should ignore them. The divorce rate is an indicator of marriages that have suffered from this inattention.

Perhaps you can use an analogy to give the women a clear picture of how important choices are in marriage. I'm picturing a tornado and its potentially devastating effects. Life (jobs, children, hardships, culture) has a way of sweeping you up into a whirlwind of chaotic activity until up, up, and away you go, wherever the cyclonic winds are driven. If you are not firmly anchored in God by focusing on Him and His Word concerning your life and marriage, and if you fail to make your marriage a priority, you might not like where life takes you. Your marriage might not even survive. Choices are important. We must choose God's best. If we don't, we choose by default.

### Loving God's Word

At the conclusion of your discussion, ask each woman, beginning with yourself, to affirm and personalize Deuteronomy 30:19:

> *Today, God has given _____ the choice between life and death, between blessings and curses. I will choose life, that me and my descendants might live!*

### First Steps for the Future

Read the First Steps at the end of chapter 12 aloud. Encourage the women to find an accountability partner who will encourage them to choose God's best for their marriage.

### Creative Touch (Optional)

Write a personal, hand-written note to each woman in your group. In the note, remind her that a beautiful wife turns to God, understands her role, and shares within a community of women. If you're willing, write down your phone number telling her you're available should she need mentoring in days to come. Personalize the note for each woman. Let her know that she is God's beautiful woman and encourage her to share what she's learned with others.

# What's Next?

I'm often asked, "What happens after we complete *The Beautiful Wife* curriculum?" Each mentor must prayerfully decide what will happen next with her group. Some ideas include:

- Continue as a mentor with a new group of women assigned by your Beautiful Womanhood coordinator.
- Keep the same group and choose a book to study from the Resources for Continued Growth appendix in *The Beautiful Wife*.
- Find a way to serve together as a group. Nothing bonds a small group together like serving. Some suggestions include helping a single mother, volunteering together at a local soup kitchen, or organizing an orphan care ministry in your church or community (see, for example, www.hopefororphans.org). A small group that I was in made sure a single woman in our town had what she needed to make a beautiful Christmas for her family. That experience changed each of us.

If your experience with the Beautiful Womanhood program has been positive, please help us start a Beautiful Womanhood wildfire across the world by letting your friends, family, and contacts know about us. I pray that as you sow good seed into others' lives, the blessing will come back to you in ways you would've never imagined!

*Sandy*